I Don't Understand Why It's Crazy
to Hear the Beautiful Songs of
Nonexistent Birds

a collection of poetry
by Philip Jason

For information contact:
Unsolicited Press
Portland, Oregon
www.unsolicitedpress.com
orders@unsolicitedpress.com
619-354-8005

Front Cover Designer: Jil Lulu Perrevoort ; Marcy Currier
Book Design: Kathryn Gerhardt
Editor: Summer Stewart

ISBN: 978-1-956692-90-7

Acknowledgments

Love Lines originally appeared in *Little Patuxent Review*

The Swan originally appeared in *Leon Literary Magazine*

The Bang of Self originally appeared in *Ganga Review*

Ode to the Panorama originally appeared in *I-70 Review*

The Circumference originally appeared in *Marrow Magazine*

Sequence of Events originally appeared in *Marrow Magazine*

Silences originally appeared in *Canary*

Escape Pod originally appeared in *The Dillydoun Review*

I grow old foolishly. originally appeared in *Delta Poetry Review*

Up into the Trees appeared in *Hawaii Pacific Review*

Praying Stones originally appeared in *Wild Gods: The Ecstatic in Contemporary Poetry and Prose*

The Dumb Grape Poem originally appeared in *Wild Gods: The Ecstatic in Contemporary Poetry and Prose*

The Orange originally appeared in *Summerset Review*

Here's what i think i would find if i found myself in hell originally appeared in *Lake Effect*

The Flies Have Become Quite Troublesome originally appeared in *Delta Poetry Review*

Remote originally appeared in the *South Florida Poetry Journal*

Present originally appeared in *Watchword*

This is what I mean sometimes when I say love originally appeared in *River and South*

Lucinate originally appeared in *The Mantle*

The Childhood that I Have Stolen from Yogi Berra first appeared in
   Superpresent

Unexpected Love: Notes originally appeared in *Delta Poetry Review*

To the Soldiering Other originally appeared in *Flare Journal*

From The Book of the Memory of the Stars originally appeared in
   Construction

Poems

4. [   ]

I Don't Understand Why It's Crazy
to Hear the Beautiful Songs of
Nonexistent Birds

hail to the starmaker,
that great light
in this saggy dream

1.

The Things You Buy are All Cheap Imitations of
the Things You Dream Of

Love Lines

I think here of famous lines. *That which once made me jealous*
now gives me an erection. It is from the Bible. And if not
the Bible, from a napkin or the heavy sand at the
sweeping ocean's edge. I remember digging my toe into
something, so if not the wet sand, perhaps your inner thigh.

I think of other famous lines. *The Equator. Mason-Dixon. Bread.*
Fishing. Pickup. I think here of waiting in famous lines,
but also of the coral reef I once cut my foot on, which,
as I looked back on it, resembled a line of poetry
I stole from the heart of another. *You are the moon, and*
I am the wolf, and between us is the howl called love.

Or if I did not steal that from the heart of another,
I ruined my own heart while producing it. Either way, I am
reminded of one more famous line: the spinal cord, running
like a coral reef between the valves of the broken
heart and the bookshelves of the ribald mind. In my
dreams, I climb yours like a beanstalk. At the top,
I find you sitting on a cloud with my heart in your hand.
Your love, you say, *is like the top half of a firefly.*

The Swan

I.
i ask the woman next to me if she remembers
the mother that held her in the bardo as she
waited for the call to return to this world
she shakes her head

I make a swan with my hand and leave
its shadow on the wall

II.
we do not remember the moment in the womb
when our tiny hearts first caught fire
but the first time that fire felt unwanted
is all we ever talk about

I make a swan with my hand and leave
its shadow on the wall

III.
I make a swan with my hand and leave
its shadow on the wall

IV.
I make a swan with my hand and leave
its shadow on the wall

V.
sometimes it feels like the avenues we
walk on those smooth crescent shaped
avenues were built exclusively for the
people we want to be in our dreams in
the instant the magician or geneticist
gets us to look away from the obvious
they are both transcendent and lonely

a swan with
my hand

its shadow on the wall

VI.
i ask the woman next to me if she will
hold me in the bardo
our tiny hearts become swans

Bad Beats

Open with the sun on that Tuesday when you never
left your house. Remember that Tuesday? You
stayed in your pajamas and watched videos
of cats puking up birthday cake.
But then came Wednesday, and that was the day
someone took a video of that rainbow with the eighth
color, and all the scientists went apeshit. The new
color, they said, was the color of a heated
Earth, the color of an Earth that was choking
on cow farts and fossil fuel breath. And you
ran out the door into the wild sprawl
of that Wednesday screaming like a hyena
and I thought: So it is,
I am afraid that I will die without ever having known
what it is like to be happy.

This is the word that comes fourth after happy.
This is the jerky motion of a joystick that controls a tiny
elf in a video game that no one has ever reached
the end of. And this is a

portal to the future: the air is hot here. Do you
remember the future? Everyone's small and lives

inside ice cubes, adrift on a sea of cola. And
the ham in this future tastes like spaghetti
and the cults here wear the rainbow's eighth color
and one day, when the sun is five billion and seven
years old, the temperature gets drunk and runs
itself buck naked into the ground
it is cold it is cold
but our thumbs are tiny and the buttons on the
reverse shrink rays are so large and

This is the world before the next world's arrival
But it's too late to know that. And this
this is the quiet that resounds at the gym
when the lights are on and you are alone
on a Monday and, for the first time, you know,
this place, its butty odors and eighth color, that's
how a zoo filled with humans would smell.

New Times Pigeon

See those ones far far over yonder, with
their armored beaks, their crude
greasy talons pulling apart the pages
of a newspaper. The pigeons have
gone mad. All day long, perched
on the edges of buildings, studying
society with their origami
brains. Snapshot! of the unsmiling people.
Snapshot! of the children being
carted around like garbage. Snapshot!
of the pigeons growing colder,
cooing indecorously, molting into
spandex. Their tiny brains yoga-pose,
producing the same thought over and
over: condo, condo, condo, condo.
And the pigeotomy, the tuning of
the heart to the talk radio stations.
The fastest learners hurled shit at the
hot dog vendors in the park for weeks
before anyone asked them to apologize.
Snapshot! of the most over yonderest,
high up in the willowy branches,
nested in lingerie snatched by the breeze.

As I walk near the lake, I see
these newsie pigeons doing calculus.
Buddy, they shout from their lacey
condos, want to play some racquetball?
Every time I hear this, I accelerate
into the panty-snatching winds.
I do not fear the ones addicted
to crumbs of meth or cocaine.
I fear the ones addicted to themselves.

Inner Sanctimoniousness

The mourning never ends. Once more I trot
the canine edges of the teeth along the shore. Breath
of snake!, overlooked wonder,

I command you into this poem! Yee lonely speck of
consciousness: No one ever thinks of what it feels like to be
breathed on by a snake.

Like a twig afloat on a sea of dirty towels, the feeling inside me,
laid out on the countertop of my soul, filleted and sweating in the
humid air. And yet, wonder eludes

the twirling gearhulk of my heart.
I bake a loaf of bread at ninety-eight point six degrees.
It is the worst loaf of bread I have ever seen.

The Bang of Self

I.

1.
I remember there being more than this
back when the parchment of this life
still smelled like a carcass.

2.
I remember the lofted galaxies
speaking to me like my body
was a language

3.
I am sure I could feel the wet ink
flowing through my veins

II.

1.
here comes an ancient clan
of village idiot emotions
decaying, false, desperate sensations

belonging to the ugly earth
where things grow backward,
into the ground toward burial

2.
All around the clan, organs
fill with fluid and chime, the
streetlamps eat shadows, pumpkins
ripen and explode and die
colors crash

3.
I am sure I could feel the words of this body
flowing through the galaxies

III.

1.
there once was a boy
who believed
the sky was full of clowns

he sang and sang
and for now, we
will let him sing

2.

We continue to let him sing

3.

And continue to let him sing.

4.

Boy of the clowns
the flame in your heart
is the one that sets the world
on fire with love.

5.

I swear I could feel the language body pulsing
I swear I once knew the carcass smell of innocent life

2.

To Those Who Sowed the Meat to this Scaffolding of Bones

Dilation

the flowers come back to the trees each year
without you having to ask.
this can make you feel irrelevant
or it can make you feel blessed.
strange how close those two things are.
strange that where there once was nothing,
there is you. Some would have you think
the universe spit you out of nowhere,
but I say it swallowed up the nothing
you once were. strange, how close
these two things are. strange
that where there once was only me
there's now also a you.
strange that all the things
have been thinking that one thought
since the first moment of this, since the moment
love was divided into two parcels: the quiet
heart and the eye. strange that when
the world comes into focus at the center
of those two things, you are overwhelmed
by what seems to be the presence of God

but is really the presence of yourself.
strange how close those two things are. strange
how every year the flowers
come rushing back to the trees without you.

Noctegenesis

I.

In this burned out forest, amongst the char pillars,
I make tribute to the ash with my urine.

II.

Sweeping back and forth, I wonder
what the ash was before the fire came
and broke that thing off from its form,
before I could have peed into it with such
moral impunity.

III.

The saddest thing I can imagine it having been
is a bird.

5.

I imagine how nature would evince the pain
of losing a bird: as a drop in temperature
or the sudden pause of a nearby rabbit; a regret
that sweeps through a distant unfired forest, causing
a single leaf on each tree to fold down the middle
exactly like a lonely hand trying to applaud the universe
for letting the bird go.

7.

I run out of urine. The ash is barely wet.
The parts of it that glisten as I shine a flashlight on them
don't look like the remains of a bird or a person
or a tree. They look like someone has grabbed
a rock of pure darkness and crushed it into dust
and sprinkled it with small drips of moonlight
from which one supposes strange mushrooms
will someday rise, puncturing that layer of darkness
as all things do in the heavy world.

Domestication

the gods (cyclonic consorts of eternity, et al, etc…)
called on you to build. you paid your workers well.
they all bought tombstones and talking refrigerators
that suggest epitaphs like (here lies a ripe one). your kids
miss you, though. the bureaucrats have supplied paperclips
that are twisted up to resemble you, but (Suzie, Johnny,
Mickey the Third) aren't fooled. you build
for your sake and not for the world in which you are
building. If you built for love, you would have built
an apple. Instead, you built a two-ton replica of
your own brain. but some of the gods (Zebo,
Nauticon, Paramhamacyde) are still
willing to save you. say these words: Now I come to you
that I might one day accept my suffering as a gift. say them
while a sugar cube melts on your tongue or the gods
won't believe you.

the gods don't believe you. maybe have your children say it
with you: Now I come to you that I might one day accept
my suffering as a gift. each of them should bear their own
sugar cube. curl your tongues around them if you are

genetically able. the words should be exiting
a tunnel of some kind or the gods won't believe you. Now

I come to you that I might one day accept my suffering as a gift.

they still don't believe you. say it with your paperclip
doppelgangers. Now I come to you… Say it in unison.
Each of you kill a butterfly and wear its wings like a
pendant. This is how it has to be; the gods
will not deny a thing that has wonder near its heart.
Now I come to you that I

the gods don't hear you. they're taking turns
down at the bureaucracy making fire out of paperclips
to give to the hunters as a joke. Sadly, the sugar
will keep you aloft for only so long. The ground is
coming at you, but you haven't had the chance to break it yet.
Your kids are willing to bear witness to your suffering,
but they aren't tall enough to be gods.

The Drift

I.
The world is not a hole into which
we shout our desires

It is an egg filled with new dreams
Flowers are reborn as flowers
Light evolves into soul

II.
and what is lost to the memories
follows us home forever

like a dog,

the call of God,
an intruder from the larger cycles,
rises up like a heartbeat
in the stones, too slow to be heard.

but every inch of abyss explored,
another inch of ourselves
explored and set right.

V.
In the kettle of the night,
the last emperor bee
stings lullabies into our skin,

driving the body
wild with new language

Ode to the Panorama

This is for the silence. This is for the space
inside us that harbors the silence, from which
the tissues and organs form. This is for
the names we give to that space: self, God, I.
This is for the self, for God and for me,
for the woodless and the disquieted. This
is for the flowers when no one is around.
This is for the body of God, from which the tissues
and organs form. This is for the stumbled,
for the self, in which the body of God sleeps,
for the dull and for the dreaded, for
the flowers when the sun is down, for the meat
when the bones are dust, for the world
as it presses its beating heart against my
cheek. This is for the colors that formed
the atoms, in which the tissues and organs
blaze. This is for the mash of life and death,
in which the night body sweats. This is for
the weapons and the salt, for the tea and
for the widow, for the tilt, for the angle,
for the mulch, the loom, the razed. This
is for the steel, for the self of the night body,
the self of love. For the blank and unwitnessed,

the I of unseen flowers, in which the tissues
and organs press back from the other side
of the cheek, in which the bone is
recommitted to the salt, in which the
silent body of God awakens from its slumber.

Every Bottom has a Bottom

I.

how, they ask, do we learn to experience beauty:
is it like how we learn to speak or walk, or
is the encompassing beauty of the world,
which we've been experiencing since birth,
diminished by hardships
to the point where what we learn
is how to remember it from time to time

II.

I don't want to be a body, dragging
a spirit behind it. I don't want
to be a body, flying a spirit like a kite.
I don't want to be a spirit either, carrying
a body on the back of my imagination

III.

all the ghosts that teach us to love our broken pieces
wander the edges of the kingdom, waiting
for the king's madness to fail.
i wait with them, more aware than ever
of the thickness of my skin,

feeling stung in the language body
by a half-heard lullaby, feeling burned
by a million useless glimpses of perfection

Scenes from the Present Moment

1.
A man encounters angels. They offer to fly him to heaven.
He says, I have a better idea. He puts chains on their ankles
and turns them into a ride

The angels carry paying customers
five feet into the sky.
Five feet

is the longest chain
the man can imagine

but the people still squeal with excitement

2.
The worms are uncomfortable
They no longer like the way we taste
when we are dead. We used to remind them
of the soil, of the earth
Now we remind them of an unpronounceable number

whose many zeros line up
like people waiting to buy cell phones

Fear not, little nightcrawlers.
We are the professional dead.
We style our hair like antennae
and when we hold
our puffy heads out the window,
we receive transmissions of love
from just beyond the heart of God

3.
Back to the angels
The delicate skin around their ankles
starts to tear.

I wish you wouldn't talk so much,
the man says to them

In the Amazon, they reply,
the jungle dreams of worms
nearly seven feet long

I Do Not Dream of Coffee

Strange as it might seem,
I remember nothing.

from before I came to this edge
of something and sang;

for your darkness to shine into
my darkness, for that pair

of orbiting darknesses to merge.
their feathery terrors…

I can barely move forward
without crumbling.

into flakes of darkness that
will lay with the earth,

or in the palm of your hand.
It takes everything;

to hold this self together.
the truth-infused self, the fire self,

it takes everything
not to slip
back into the beggar-self.

to whom the now shining darkness
is just sadness or betrayal.

or the world toward which
the lonely madness;

inside us screams
its mating calls.

Stasis Fire

Tonight, like most others,
it is hard to sleep
because you are fluorescent
when you dream. I gently drag
the dull edge of my fingernail between
the two most prominent freckles
on your left shoulder.

From where I am lying on the bed,
I count the meager gathering of stars
visible through your window, lamenting
this horrible angle I've found. You said
fire is cold because it's remorseless
and hungry. I am certain I have told you this
before, but you always say you're not to blame
for the kind of light your dreams
now produce. This is the age
of technology! you say, the age of the
mechanical soul! Happiness (your favorite
word when we argue) is the old
way; the new way: form a crust around

the heart, protect our stained emotional glass
from pitiless pop music.

Starbucks opens a location in this poem
and begins to serve coffee to the people
who've come looking for transcendence.
Written on every cup, the same forty letters:
If fire was only remorseless it would be boring.
This is what it has come to.

This is what the end always looks like in the
end. The world stops decaying, the words
on the side of a coffee cup
make you buzz like a long white lightbulb.

I sit up in your bed and shift my hips.
Nothing changes. The good angles burned away
when we reentered the atmosphere. The good
angles all lost their wings. It breaks
the stained glass of my heart to say this
but we never should have died.
We never should've fallen from
the way up there back into these bodies.

3.

Allow Me to be Brave Without Causing Damage

The Circumference

every circle is perfect on the good days.
and there are no bad days, God
tends to the circles like the bee tends to the flower, and
everything that God learns while studying
inside me becomes a circle in paradise.
and there are no bad days. But
on the bad days,
God lights a cigarette and blows rings of smoke
into the abyss; everything inside me that God
struggles to understand becomes
a cigarette burn on some delicate
tapestry or eyelid, and somewhere in paradise
a circle fills with milk and darkness
and hardens into an eye.

On the good days,
when God studies inside me, the cigarettes
sit quietly on the edge of a piano and the
pianos sit quietly on the edge of the self,
and there is no self; the day shines
and the pianos do not sing, they listen to themselves
being quiet, listen to the hum of the resting wood and feel
the divinity of life. But

on the bad days,
when God brings fire and sits at the pianos, on
the days when God lights
a cigarette and plays the pianos, plays only
the long, temperamental songs
from the opera of the soul, on those days the self
curls. The end of the self, where on the good days
God studies the circumference of God, reaches
back to the self's beginning and the cigarettes
burn. On those days, the smoke drifts

through the air like the self on a bad day, and
there is one less circle in paradise, a new eye
opens and shines like the keys of a piano
after they've been licked by the delicate
fingers of God; the eye shines from
beginning to end, and there is no end, it
shines like the keys of a piano, like a garden
during a summer performance of the opera of the soul,
and in that garden, the bees tend the flowers like
God tends to the circle, and the good day finds
its beginning in the bad, and everything
is studied, and everything is learned,
and there is no fire, and there is no self and
every circle is perfect on the good days.

Escape Pod

X tries to unlove someone after the heart has opened.
A billion stars, I say. A billion

stars
Have tried to unlove the loved, they have torn themselves into
holes trying and

into them now tired light seeps and into them tired light seeps
And therein, (there or in the cavity of your chest, X) tired light
cracks

its knuckles, breaks its thin bones seeking respite from godliness.

Sequence of Events

1.
In the kingdom of air, all things
are braided. The air is passed between us
like a thread. The air is passed from plants
to us like a thread. The air is passed from
earth to sky like a

2.
In the kingdom of air

4.
Once there was a prince who sold his own mother
to a foreign power. He asked for a single
gold coin. He fed that coin
to the payment slot of a pinball machine
and let each of the balls slip
effortlessly between the flippers and into the hole.

5. In the kingdom of air, another list of things
that twinkle in the disquieted
light: butter, twigs, the shell of a turtle
coated in fresh honey.

6.
Sometimes I wonder
what would
make me feel more alone:
being the only person in a parade
being the only person
watching as a parade goes by

7.
In the kingdom of factories, the machines
gather to breathe. The air is a braid. The air
is a fluid braid pulsing in sour lungs.

8.
Anointed boy, cherry-bearer, sugar of the sun,
these are the names the mother gave to the prince
as she pumped him full of nutrients

X. In the kingdom of air and factories,
the pollution comes not from the factories
but from the dreams that factories come from.

11.
Sometimes I wonder if I'm ever really alone.

Y.
Another list, more disquietude: Elephant
collections, Margarine as an answer
in a game of charades, Half turn of a wrench

13.
This poem was designed to end whenever you want it to.
I should have told you earlier.
I should have done so many things.
I should have kept that gold coin.

14.
In the kingdom of factories and loneliness, a mother
remembers the nutrient-rich machine she called her son
"Take this honey," she says to the turtle sitting on her lap
"bring it to the dreams the factories come from,
bring it back to God."

15. Sometimes I

16.
In the kingdom of air and sometimes,
everything is a pulse between two moments.
The plants are a braid, the dreams are a braid,
the disquiet is a braid cursed in sugar,
holding the lungs like a hand.

Up into the Trees

I will always remember that night
when you told me you were never going
to die, that your father had been a god

before his retirement. In that
line of work, you said, immortality
is like a healthcare plan; or like

a pension for years of tossing
lightning bolts and impregnating
unsuspecting women with demigods.

I said: anyone I would know? you
said, what? I said, the demigods,
your sisters and brothers, surely

some of them are famous? you
laughed and cracked your knuckles
against the wooly skin of that coconut

I bought for you from a guy
who climbs trees for a living. him?
I said, the climber, I believe he climbed

the tree with only one hand, his other
wrapped around the ivory handle
of the large rusted tooth he used

to hack the fruit from the palms
and crack the shell.
It sounded like thunder, I said,

so maybe him? But you didn't want to
talk about your father's indiscretions
or your mother's constant sadness

and vengeful tantrums. We watched
the sun as it fell into the ocean,
melting the waves, the seagulls

leaping away from the instability
with bits of stolen foam. I think
I met your father once, I said, he

was there to catch me when I fell
from the tree I climbed too early,
before I knew you could ever want

something from the trees, before
I knew what it was like
to remember things without you.

You laughed again, laughed exactly
like you do when you bleed
from my memories into the place in my head

where I wonder if you kept that promise,
if you're living the life of forever
somewhere in the heavens,

cracking open stars with the blade-side
of your hand, drinking milk
directly from your mother's heart.

Silences

not too long ago, curious people sat around and stared
at things in solitude. there was nothing to read. no one
to worship. there was the self they knew in silence. there
were the questions that rose up from the inexplicable. they
contemplated patiently and gave up. there was nothing
to know and they were satisfied. then came the printing press
and a new kind of silence. at night, some recalled the old ways.
then someone invented the lightbulb and smothered the stars.
then television. then pop stars filled the atmosphere. then the
mind became a pop star. then there was so much sadness and
weight loss. then good silence died. then the bees
found a way across the universe and didn't say goodbye.
they left behind just enough honey for us to fight over and
a third kind of silence. no one realized that we loved the bees.
it wasn't in any books. it wasn't even waiting for us to notice.
it was something that was there for us if we wanted it, like
a silent telephone of the heart that knows exactly who to call
the moment you pick up the receiver. you can use it
to call someone in the old way. the calls don't cost anything,
but if you talk too much, you become disconnected.

The Odd Miracle

I have seen something
as often as I have seen nothing.
                    - the Future

even the observant miss most things.
even the *keenly* observant.
the world is big,
the universe a shapeshifter.
at best, we can prune delights

from the cascade.
at best we can prune *keenly*.
but this is enough.
Even one miracle,

even one ordinary moment testifying
to its own miraculous occurrence;

even a single sock,
dangling from a clothesline
sustains the spirit that dreams of the body;

even a paperclip rusting in a field
is shaped like something,
even if that something is only itself.

Homesong

I.
In a memory from my childhood
I connect two cups with a string, put a cup
to my ear and listen for that joy

II.
I can't understand the man who speaks
into the other's cup.

III.
I feel creeping, at the edges of my light,
coiled disappointment: Here comes
the muting of the ocean's blue and the last
delicate roar of the earthworm.

IV.
Frantically, I pull the cup I hold
close to my heart.

V.
if at this point the string is plucked
by either hand of child or latent

heart of man within, the shrieking
tension that it holds will empty

VI.
into the air

VII.
a single soft note.

VIII.
I feel this too: the coming of the wind
to carry that note in its pores, and
the angels of home to mourn as the note
passes through their feathery wings;

IX.
and the churn of the soil beneath
the calloused feet of the seasons
as every childhood, whether lost
or still held, repeats itself, searching
for the song the note belongs to.

several words at the end of a personality:

A train horn rips through the night air
to signify that a thing is passing. Threads of light
trickle down from the starry miasma, and I
can't separate myself from the absence
that certainly some of the stars must be made of.
Not all heaviness is explained by gravity. In the end,
the person is zeroed out because truth demands it.
Truth demands this as well:
We are all waiting for our parents to die so we can
say the things we want to say.
No one confesses to being the common man. When
we count the people in a room, we forget
to count ourselves. Such is the trauma
of the metaphor, hallowed be. I think I hear
the thunder of training wheels. I think
a bird's departing soul
is ripping through the night air like a train horn.

I grow old foolishly.

every step of life takes me farther
into the abyss, my bones

filled with outdated information
from my youth, my organs filled

with juvenile love letters written
on beautiful, handcrafted

pieces of paper. my memories
assail me with pitchforks, angry

because each of them,
before it was a memory,

was promised it would be the truth.

II.
the memories of stars, full and beautiful in the sky
(until I put them inside me to light some masturbation
fantasy),

are particularly ruthless. they aim eyeward, never
for the heart, riding memories of the wind, cloaked
in memories of my parents. they look like angels
rising from a fall, like leaves in autumn
sailing away from the earth, like

III.
Memories, I know, are always Godless,
always the opposite of love. they are
life that has been tranquilized by time.

but *these* memories. so so full of light.
the twinkle of their fury so visible as they
come for their vengeance. the howl,
the smell of burning coal,
my younger self strapped to a coffin before them,
raging toward me like a missile.

Modern Everlasting

before the world was modern it was just
people at play in a heaving darkness is what
they tell us, we have learned from our
mistakes they say as they stand
on these gross pulpits made of steel bones
and arched troglodyte backs, we have
learned from our grievous mistakes and made
the new gods mortal we have etched
some code into the genes of the apple and now
the apple in its pearly redness in its hallowed
red paper skin becomes a symbol
for sin that won't embarrass us when
it shows up in our children; more importantly
we have found a way to live in harmony
with the absence of nature and each other

before we can ask them if they mean the absence
of each other or actual each other
they ask us to hooray.

i hooray

before we can ask them why there is a space
inside us that no one talks about a not so hallowed
space that feels both modern and also like
people at play in a heaving darkness; a space
that feels like dead apples sleeping apples waiting
waiting waiting for their genes to stop hurting a
space filled with bones and rotting flesh the
pickled bones and putrid pockmarked flesh of
our mortal gods; filled with nicknames
for friends we do not have and sins we are
only now creating for the first time like
market penetration and data slurping and reality puns;
before we can ask them why the sockets of their
eyes are filled with bright white teeth, they
mount their turbo spouses and gallop off

no one asks, but I hooray

4.

[   ]

Bird Song

I.
a cloud that always looks like my father,
hovering in the sky, the same
expression on its face, the same
curl in its fingers,

never raining or growing larger.

and yet,
I am the one who is crazy
for hearing the beautiful songs
of nonexistent birds.

II.
the half-illuminated face of God
crashes down on us from
the trees, splitting
the trunk of the body shell

The pious think it funny.

For every truth, they say,
a corresponding piece of darkness;
for every chance to love, a
fear of dying. For

every burst of rage,
a beautiful full moon, vulnerable
to disregard;

For every eye,
a lid.

III.
but! the diet fiends counter,

what flows in our veins
is more than blood

it is the *dream* of blood…

IV.
in grass so tall it must be weeping,
the body shell blushes and emits

a sound like the friction of cricket legs
wildly kindling a summer day's heat

I open my mouth.
the song of the birds inside me escapes,
joining itself
to the open mouth of the sky

To Every Person I Will Never Know Existed

in the distance between us
God dreams of flowers.

Praying Stones

The stone that sits beneath
the willow tree in your front yard
is praying to be a stone.
All it does is pray to be a stone.
For it, every moment
is the same. It prays and prays,
and the universe answers its prayer.

The universe prays too.
When the universe prays, it prays
to be you.
Every moment for you
is different. Some are happy and
some are sad.
but the prayer never changes.

One day,
you will see the weeping self
laid down beside the praying stones.
Even then,
as the worms of the heavens
chew your spirit
into the furious void,

the universe
will continue its prayer.
It will never stop praying to be you.
If you listen right now,

you can hear the atoms
cradling to their breasts
the pious syllables of your life.

Song for a Heart Union

For Cori and Kelly

Of this we've only just begun to speak,
this true, this sacred rise, this
slaying of our lazy doom, this full,
this blossom, this glimmering stem.
Of this, we've only just begun,
this now, this here, this gianting
of soul, this word, written slow,
this body, this fold, this
electric whimsy in the limbs.
Of this we've only just begun!
Make way! Make way!
Let the salamander dream, let air,
let the trees which have come
from far over there, let the sun
that has been circling impatiently
above, let the moon, let the stars,
let their emissary light;
let the rain, let the worms, let the birds
carouseling in the sky, let the stones,
let the nerves, let the marbling
in the eyes, let the crust of the bread, let
the mold, let the bark of trees ignite,
let the darkness regurgitate

the undying light, let the night come,
let it shimmer, let it glide,
let gloom of breath hereby subside, for
we are gathered here today, the spirit
and its many forms, for this, this true,
this sacred, this rising of the heart.
For that, make way! Let howling foam!
Let rust. Let angels and their toads. Let
more, let every, let plum and bone. Of
this risen heart, we have only just begun.

psalm for the gland of consciousness

what within you thing
belongs to each other thing

in every word you release from captivity,
let me hear, as I do in every animation of your hands,
the soliloquy of God that is your life.

let every prayer be a thing for each other thing:
that those vessels, may they find a way to gently graze
within me, that I will find a humble way into them to blaze.

and the spirits of your teeth, the rotting particulars
of your past, the unsanitized dreams of your ancestors
loose like the heat that you are right now letting drift
unprofitably through the room you are in;

but all the words that spiders build their homes to catch.
falling from your eyes,
setting, like fire, the silver webs to glisten.

Apparition

Weary lover. I know you are tired, tired like
the grip of the ocean around the drowned,
the grip of the wind around

the birdless wing; but be still. Be still
and put your skittish light on us
like God put those radiant knuckles
on to your soft hands.

Do not hide from yourself.
I have seen the forces
that sent the wild galaxies tumbling
riding on inside you,

in your sense of humor
and bright eyes.

Be at peace. be at so much peace
it scares you. Come undone.
Walk through the valley of the shadow
of self. bring that light with you. put it
to the heavens,

let it grow,
let it bloom.
let it scab;

then open up
and let the wonderful new stars
grab you where the shame is holding on.

When the Imperfect House of Your Body Contains the Knowledge of Perfection

Even then the joy inside you
remains on course to witness
the everlasting angle of its own ascent,
the self of the body
therefore always on the verge
of destruction, the self of the soul
always on the cusp of rising
from its cocoon. Unlike the worm
which gives up its body to become
wings for the butterfly, the soul
gives up its wings to become the body
of the universe. There is no despair;
there is metamorphosis, sacrifice,
expansion of the sacred edges,
a place where two roads converge
in the mind. On one walks a horde
of drunken angels, returning home
from celebrating God; on the other
a troop of sober demons
returning from the sulfur forges
where light is made. Life
to the angels is television, to

the demons it is toil. As they meet,
traditions break: love
ceases to be cleft into good and evil,
your darkness stops weeping,
it no longer bleeds its wonder
into the darkness of the other.
There's no despair. There is what you
have forgiven, drive, purpose,
the half open hands on the back
of the soul grasping clawishly at
the air, the flowers they will become
when at last the body has risen.

The Dumb Grape Poem

there is no art, there is no love. the stars that rage
and shove each other through the heavens are balls
of dust and that dust is also meaningless. the ground
is dumb, the moon is dumb, the raisin is still a grape
and the grape is dumb. if there is nothing after death,
we are here before this place is ripe; we haul
grape-dumb bodies through an unfinished world,
the unhinged stars shine their light on the undone.
if there is nothing after death, love does not teach itself
to the people we become. the Earth merely sputters hot
slime from its volcanic pores and the conversation
you just had already smells like rotting milk. the sky
is dumb, the rain is dumb, dumb is art, dumb is love;
the heavens beat their stupid drums as the stars
rage and shove us deeper into the bones we haul.
if there is nothing after death, the wings of birds
molest the stingy winds, the candle is a sore
that rages out its light. if there is nothing after death,
we wait impatiently for the world to be done, for ships
to bring the grapes, for the television's hum, for love
to raise the dust into stars and sail them through the
dumb. if there is nothing after death, the songs we sing
are sour milk, the truth we seek is sour milk, the bones

we haul are sour milk, and the death that waits for us to die
howls its milky breath into the unhinged light
as we trawl the meaningless and stupid night for love

5.

*You Who Have Conquered the World Meet Me
Where Your Heart was Broken*

The Orange

The orange just organizes itself into an orange
and is then at peace.
I eat the peaceful orange,
it becomes part of me. I give to it
an equal share of my broken heart.
Slowly, it discovers rage.

Here's what i think i would find if i found myself in hell

everything i ever thought i wanted. in hell,
i have to see what it's like to fulfill all my desires.
the devil is standing over me, shouting encouragements
as i discover one at a time that all the realities in the world
never live up to the magnitude of my desire for them.
all the while, i am trying to figure out how to leave
without wanting to be somewhere else. where is
heaven, i ask? and the devil answers, the devil
even shows me the way.
i start to suspect the devil
is being sincere:
he wants me to get there, wants me to go;
his hell is having to watch soul after soul suffer
because they don't know how to stop.
i feel sorry for him. i want him to be free.
instantly, i see: he *is* free.
the story about how he battled God and fell from heaven
is nothing more than a dream that overtook him.
being rundown by a dream like that is also how i got here.
i want to tell him this,
but the world still turns above
and i am not yet dead enough for that kind of courage.

In Regard to Your Happiness

1. On viewing others as they see themselves

let's be honest: people are disenchanted creatures
habitually bad imaginers, genetically poor
imaginations, imaginations strained through
coarse filaments, and it would be a disservice
to the entire human iterance to yada yada yada...

2. On viewing others as we view ourselves

The problem here is that we, the under-
viewed, view ourselves as we wish the others
would view us—let them call such nonsense
omnibus retrotraction—a mathematically
hollow function, we input the future and
are returned the past we were trying
to circumvent; and we—I speak of the daring
we, not the trifling we, as in "we are acrobats"
and not "we are summarized in topiary"—
do not want the past to be solved any more
than we want the future to preclude us.

3. On other methods of observation

I could see you as a reflection in the mirror,
a rather ruthless viewing, or as a constellation
of bones and organs, platonically, or I
could remove you entirely to the sand dunes. You
could be a corporation, for therein the surge
of life is grotesque and swollen, and you could be
a murder or a crust of bread, for similar reasons.

4. On, just on

Back and forth we go, arguing about what
is or is not loitering in the reflective shell
of the eyes, but it's all so fucking pointless.
Once you let it, the universe takes you
into its palm and grinds you to a paste, rolls
the paste of you into a ball and carves a smile.
Happiness loves the plastic spirit; loves *your*
plastic spirit, so take a deep breath, make room
in your heart for the long, gorgeous fall.
Try not to shit yourself on the way down.

Awakening Part 1

Every doubt I have ever had
suddenly wants a name. I
don't know that many names.
Let me name the animals, the stars,
the numbers. Let me
name the snowflakes, the different lives
of the atoms in my body.

Is it not the purpose of this poem
to release a joy
from some prison or some debt or
some unpleasant conversation? Is it not why
my doubts want names, so they won't
be embarrassed when the joy is released
and they stand before it? But there is no one
to name my doubts. I am a sinkhole. The world
is ready for the heat I produce, has been
drinking that heat since the day I was born.

Sun, come up and be read! Pass and
be sorrowed. The universe is
something everywhere but inside me.

Smart Mouth

I remember a lullaby sung to me
by somebody: la la la
a million fucking words about love
and not a single thing has changed

Still, I cannot fathom being
untouched by the suffering of others.

la la la la
every piece of bread you eat remembers me
every thank you
that has softened the shield around your heart
has passed through my lips.

I cannot fathom it, i
cannot fathom the space between
one ether and another

if all the light in the universe
is a single thread
how do we dream of anything
but love?

Ongoing Catalog of Sin and Sobriety

I.

every child comes to this life
carrying an idea
that will bring abiding peace
to the already here

and the language we offer them
lacks just enough words
to make them sound like idiots
when they try to share it

II.

time and time again
the great visionaries will create
enormous palaces and a wake
in which will ride
people of ill desire and high aspiration
who come to congregate in the glorious halls
and shit in all the corners

III.

our doubts shall have
the finest homes

better food than us, better friends
they will bathe and they will be
the cleanest doubts

IV.
we will finally feel it

as the world succumbs
to our inventions:
deep within the heart,

the sigh of a balloon
as it slips
from the hand of a child

the roaring glow of disappointment
summoned when
the clowns eat the pie

The Flies Have Become Quite Troublesome

The past is a grave filled with me.
Death is the wings of the angel
who wears my body in this world.
I want to believe there is an escape.
I want to believe that if I choose
the right words, God will find them
and make a home there. But
God has chosen the words already.
My enormous wings will take me
to them when the time comes.
Till then, I wait, the fool inside
the angel, who could not see death
when I was a child, could not see it
even when I was a younger man.
Now it is present in all my memories.
Everyone I've ever known stands beside
a sighing river, washing their bones,
hanging the best ones up to dry.

Remote

Oh great mother, microwaver of hearts, turn
your television on. You are the sun now, and I
the remote control device. Please don't
push the button marked "Paralyze Soul." That
button is a mistake, a modification made
by marketing fiends–gurus of the fat brain–and the
crows that pick at the crumbs that fall from the white
Formica countertops of their eyes. Oh great
mother, parking spot of kindness and information,
turn your closet lights on. It is winter now,
season of salt and movie stars, season
of the long night; it is time to burn calories
in the fiery lakes of our cells. Please, tend well
the snowman who sits at the gates
of the deli. He meditates on the heroin addict
nature of God and knows in each
of the one-of-a-kind snowflakes of his brain
that I long to be larger than the troubles that
feed me, that some of us long to grow beyond
these stinking bodies, that we are all forecasted
to die crazy and alone. Oh great mother,
high-speed ceiling fan of the holy trinity
of cause, effect and mercy, turn your pancakes

over. They are starting to burn and I
am the flesh of burning pancakes, injecting
heaven into my bridgeless veins. I can feel
the heat of self-pleasuring bacteria coming
from your lips as you press them to my
forehead. This must be the day when the garbage
man finally comes for me. This is the day when
the jugglers and Port-o-potty salesmen come
and take me away. Oh great mother, meat slicer
of the reason why it so often seems
a thing can't be itself and be loved at the same
time, turn your head, please, take my hand,
hold it in your throat, save me, save me
from the open pores of banking and investment.
All I want is to see the universe's kindness
in everything. All I want is for you to silence
the pudding pop commercials that run in my
head without permission. All I want is a blessing
for these asphyxiated plums that have
hardened into knuckles because someone
forgot to eat them. All I want is for you to
put your gun down and give me a name.

Hero Complex

Sometimes, I imagine you
as both otherworldly and helpless, a tendril
of light caught in the branch of a tree.
I open myself to you with the fatty organs
of my arrogance, but you leave me
stranded on the ground, waiting
with outstretched arms.
You, who brings edges
to the better known hand of God
so that one day, when I am ready,
I can fall off and be caught by the other
hand; you, whose need for a hero
has atrophied, setting me to drift
like an oil spill. See the clever luster
I bring to the waters. When they are placid,
I'm a slick of radiant darkness, shielding you
from the ocean floor. When wild, floated grief;
I am tumbled by the drowning birds.

Present

everyone present pretends to be yesterday
drinks in hand,
watching the bubbles become ordinary air again

in the other room,
portraits of death stalk the nonbelievers

the people party on
some are witty
some look like cotton where their eyes should be
the universe expands as they sign contracts

a toast is shaken from the atmosphere
"all light is trapezoids! all weather is quality!"

as these words are drifting,
a shadow vanishes into someone's breaking heart
no one seems to care

maybe they are breathing too much to notice
maybe their diets make them slow

maybe they are dreaming of somewhere else
and all of this is just what grows where no one really is

maybe to them this is life
and everything is ignorance while the stars exhale

Through the Glass Jelly

Down the street, three children
draw on the sidewalk
with fat pieces of chalk. They draw
corporate logos, Golden arches and
the other new symbols for infinity;
they draw images from
popular advertisements, their
favorite catch phrases ("Uh
oh, I'm having an emotion!"),
billionaires.
"Celebrity," they say with their eyes,
"has swallowed up the magic
that once belonged to the
sun, the moon, the breaths we take.
And though the world, through reflex,
still produces flowers and wind,
the smiles of children and starry nights,
it is a graveyard yearning to be a wasteland."

Down the street, three teenagers
draw attention to themselves, hoping
that the light they do not absorb
winds up on television, hoping

that the light they do not absorb
will crack the glass of their reality
and let in something special,
the fiery bush of personality,
which will tell them at last
how to dream, how to chisel their
desires into stone, how to codify and name
their feelings, those meaningless
feelings that beg for validation,
that want so badly to appear
in passport photos, that wait in the
shadows for someone who wants
their autograph.
"Hey," they say, the teens,
"that belongs to me." But never
do they specify, not through glance
nor even quickened respiration,
what thing it is
what thing around which
the soft grip of their hearts has turned to stone.

Down the street, three forty-somethings
draw the following conclusion:
that all things once deemed hopeless
have been given new hope by
the bloom of technology, which
has reached into the human mind

like how vines reach into long abandoned
buildings, like how vines replace
the vacancy of abandoned buildings
with fresh matter, with the hum of
brand new molecules, fresh
molecules and the unbridled, joy-filled
screams of their whirling electrons.
"Thanks to technology," the grownups say,
"we can feel the happiness of matter
in ways that we never could before
feel the happiness of ourselves."
And the descent of the cascading skin
as their eyelids
lay themselves like blankets
over the glass jelly of the eyes
dismisses the light that falls from the sparkling sun
while it dangles on the hook of the sky.

Down down down, three octogenarians
draw upon experience, draw
upon it like the drag of smoke
through the filaments of
a cigarette butt. They say, "Yes,
we once were children,
not so lost, we knew the stars,
knew the stars but not
how far away they were; and once,

we were teens, we were teens
who knew the ache but not the cause,
knew the growing pains of the tight
immortal soul as the mortal shell
grew too fast inside it; and once,
we were grownups
and then we knew the cause,
the cause but not the ache, we knew
in terms of which celebrity, which face, which
bright, shining brand
just how far away from us
are those blessed stars, those
spectacular gravity engines which produce
the fresh and screaming molecules,
the fire of our personalities, the song, the song, etc…
Now, with tired skin and broken-knuckled
joints, we come to the long awaited
destination, we come to that fixed point
in the distance, our hands
are open, ready to close
the gully between self and star, ready
for one last taste of humming wonders.
We are shining, we are bright,
and this is what we find:
we find the end is missing,
the famous end just simply isn't there."

6.

And Yet We Come Here Expecting to Feel Alive
in these Tiny Finite Boxes

Eclipse

sometimes grief is elliptical
sometimes the stars are not on fire
sometimes the chastity of the amoeba
makes the trees feel shame

sometimes i see you
sometimes you are the holes
in a snowflake or
the caves in a mountain

sometimes the desert island
longs for a shipwreck

and the tree is ashamed

sometimes we laugh
sometimes we cry
sometimes we cry into our knuckles

sometimes we cough ourselves open
to the dust of cold stars
and the weight inside us grows hands
and tries to fly away

This is what I mean sometimes when I say love

The slowly heating darkness
buried in the heart of a pile of leaves

The wild younglings always come for it.
I am prone to look away from its destruction.
What a disappointing thing it is
to watch the exposure of that center.

Or any center like it.
I bet the first person to open a body
was disappointed to discover

the slimy organs
holding each other like children do
when they hide in a closet from thunder

and not a gateway
to the throne room of God
or a circus of writhing shadows
or a mirror.

The Grind

I.

Beyond the lights from the city, the animals
go to die. They remember tiny fragments
of a sonata they once overheard.

II.

Rejoice! The powers that surround us
grind us down into a different kind of light.
The lightless light of starless futures
in which everything is the dust of everything.

III.

The term that higher forms use for us
is "warrior-slaves." Our only choice
is whether or not we will make
the same mistake twice.

IV.

The lightless light of our future calms
the tender edges of piano-playing nerve
cells. The animals are drawn by the song
to return from death and enter the old

light of the city. The smell of their fur
completes an allegory in which the animals

V.

Those awful powers grind us down into
our least favorite mistake. They grind us
into twitching packets of nerves
that slowly remember how to be light.

VI.

Light was our first mistake.

VII.

I lied. We do not get to choose.

Megalomenius

we are all trying to remake the world
in our own image.
the instincts of God are inside us
like the instincts of ants are inside the ants.
the true cause of suffering is
the feel of the world in our mouths
as our teeth press down; we chew because
the still jaw reminds us of death.
were we to die though
we would instantly remake ourselves
in the image of ourselves.
the instincts of God are like that.
they are inside us like worms are inside
the intestines of a dog. the writhe
of creation propels us forward while
things content with their resting inertia dream
of a single omnivorous moment of grace.
And so I know that God also dreams
of such a moment; the instincts of God
are like that. The instincts of God are
inside us like our fingerprints are
all over the inside of God. Everything
is symmetry or feels like a cycle. Everything's

a reflex or well-lit memory. For instance:
I remember once being left behind
by the forces leaking out of me.
Never before had I been alone
with the trees or the moon. Never before
had I been alone with my heart. Sometimes,
fear and love are not fighting over
the disposition of God. Sometimes,
the ants are quiet and we can hear them dream.

The Clouds are Imitating that Face You Made at Last Year's Costume Party

You were dressed like my mother, your hair
dyed the color of a distant galaxy, a tunic of stars
hanging from your eyes, a song of prosperity
trailing behind you like a shadow, even when
we walked through the mud, even then. You
said only one thing to me that night: you told me
that you'd never seen the ocean, had never even
held a seashell to your ear or drank a glass
of water that someone had put salt in as a joke.
You cried when you said that. A single tear
ran down what looked to me like my mother's
face. I took it from you with my finger, put it in
my mouth, put my head into the valley of your hands,
and you held it like a stone, held it close to your ear,
hearing for the first time the slow breathing
of the trees, the inhalation of the energetic dust the
suns' knuckles kneaded out of less exciting matter;
and the sound beneath that sound, the words
my father hid from my mother inside me, small
words, the smallest in the world, each of them
an ocean, each of them a long, breaking bone.

Lucinate

a star shouts across the universe
for ten billion years and is extinguished.
on the next day, the star appears in my sky
for the first time. happy birthday star! it shines
like something that will not know it has died
for ten billion years. for ten billion years,
death will be chasing it at the speed of light,
it will only whisper in the sky.
and just like this ignorant new light, i think i
am an ancient star, alive and shouting.
are we both wrong? i don't remember being
born. one day, i appeared on this side of the universe.
maybe i was extinguished long ago and
what i am now is an echo being chased by death.
maybe like that ancient star, i appear over and
over again throughout the universe, living an existence
that seems loud and fresh to me, always thinking
i am like a star on fire with life,
but always an echo, always a whisperer.

7.

In the End, You Go Mad or You Go Free

Awakening Part 2

In these many years, I have seen
the loneliness of being human;
I have spoken hopefully of it
to the lonely others
only to see in their eyes
not recognition
but that loneliness growing bolder.
Now, my doubts, quivering,
nameless and afraid,
try to name themselves.
They rage like drifting cinders, reach
for the far away stars
with their tiny claws. But I,
in love of myself,
have walked with the drums
of that regret, have tasted
the song of the plum, the blush
of clean air;
have gone on long enough to see
the impermanence of all things
radiating from every center,
and, as I lay these words

down on the page,
I feel not the presence of God,
but the life inside of God that is me.

Séance

all the songs I sing in tribute
to the othering of I, the
etceterization of personal things,
the removal of the toys of self
that we, as children, played with
during the fever stages of life.
great lover in the sky, watching
as we play ourselves to death,
sing with me in that brilliant voice,
that funeral voice rich with joy;
something somewhere sometime
must be building us a way
back into the fevered light.

Replay

in my memories you
are a memory with a body
unaware that the love you feel
is just a memory

I am warmed by your innocence
I do not remember the spiders
so together we laze and watch
the spider webs
form in the hands of God

The Childhood that I Have Stolen from Yogi Berra

He pauses at the lip of the darkness. Love,
he says, is the fire in which the self is fire.
He lunges at the dragon, dreams of grass
along the blithe Italiano coast. Yogi
quotes the starlight, rages rages rages
'gainst the batting cage of life. His voice
is soft, attention focused on the jewel
between his eyebrows. His mother
tucks him into bed, puts an apple
in his bag. She writes him love notes, which
I steal, whose sentiments I steal: Dear
Lorenzo, Mio Bambino, The dragon in my heart
speaks only of my love for you. Love, it says.
Is the fire in which the self is fire is the sun
inside the mother is the teeth before which
the darkness curls. In its mouth, the jewel
of consciousness twinkles, in its eyes,
the lunge begins; he dreams of salted grass,
rages rages rages like a flame.

The Missing

on the beach you find
a puzzle piece in the sand
and wrap it in your palm; you do not
look for any others. I say

somewhere out there is someone
searching for this missing piece.
doesn't that remind you of God?
this, you say,

is the only piece *not* missing;
that's why it reminds me of God.

For the first time,
I see your secret, that you
just like I, are an angel
sent here by God
to find the missing angels, who are

us. it is the way of God,
you tell me,

to make everything its own salvation;
we exist in perfect proportion: One soul,
one person to save it. Then you turn

to the horizon, throw the piece
into the salted waves. We watch
as it completes the ocean. The water
holds it perfectly.

Eminence

When I die, my eyes will go out
but the light will remain;
that's love when I imagine death.
Love when I think of life is a world without fear,
a world in which the heart is large enough
to traverse inconceivable distances.
To see such a world is easy.
One need only look up at the night sky.
The stars there are so far apart
but they still seem so close to each other.

All Blooming

every secret that it harbors in its
well-worn passages, a soul, a soul flowering
in the love that binds it to the labyrinth.
Note how your own petals lay themselves across
the seams of your binding in so gentle a pattern.
That is the face of the Godlife, hand on the
crank, cranking the lever of blossoms,
solving the maze.

Unexpected Love: Notes

My close friend confides in me that she feels
joy when she farts at the pompous
students during a yoga class.
Strangely, this makes me think about
the different forms of love. Love, the defeat
of the colossus. Love, the end of the universe
resting in a pouch on the side of the heart, etc.
My friend is wild about these forms of love,
which of course, just another form. Love,
the wildness of your friend as she rages
in the smallest way against a tyranny
smaller than the rage. Love, the act of rage
that brings unexpected joy to a friendship.
Love, the misdelivered parcel kept safe
by the lunatic who receives it...
I could go on and on like this.
The describing of love is an art form,
widely studied and elucidated on
by the practitioners of yoga. They say
innumerable ways exist to describe
the describing of love. One for each
of the times someone has found a new way
to love the strangers in their yoga class.

One for each of the different wilds secured
in a pouch on the side of my friend's heart.
One for each heart that has ever opened
to something that does not belong to it,
for each creak of that opening heart. One for
each of the glorious days that joy
has been misdelivered into my hands,
the days when I see love rumbling
through everything. Love, the phantom
limb of every madness. Love, the salt
in the eye of evil. Love, the gorgeous
misdeed that hangs adoringly in the air.

To the Soldiering Other

Forgive me if I place this on you like a kiss
placed upon the forehead
of someone who fears darkness
by someone who loves them
but you are more than a friend,
you are a totem in which a piece of my heart is stored;
and though we are not birds,
together we can plagiarize their existence.
As we rise, I will whisper in your ear:
Yes, it's true, if God
forgets to create gravity, the angels can't fall,
but snowflakes fall too and somehow
know to stop themselves
before they get to hell.

The Ant on the Floor Searching for Crumbs Doesn't Seem Lonely

Billions of people and I
the search for love
as we dream it is
never hollow
never say hello hi
how is your dream of love
never friends and
neighbors but
we dwell in the
search for love and
a breath of uncrumpled air
a look of sky…
love is a crumb
searching for ants
we dream
a crumb of soul
searching for a dream
to carry it on its back

The Opera

Act 1

I.

I wish to scribble a few sentiments
before the words we use have lost their meaning
Even now, if I speak of the stars, many people
look at the little pieces of light that hang in the sky
and not inside themselves
where the stars are personal and therefore real

II.

I understand the sorrowful call of the gulls
my mortality has encased them in a name
they retain the gift of flight
but the joy it once held for them
belongs now to my struggle.

III.

all we ever wanted was to know
the song inside our parents' hearts
all we ever heard
was the salt trapped in icebergs

Act 2

I.

The whole world wears
my face when I am angry
It also wears my face
when I'm in love.
Fickle world,
how can I trust you
if your heart is my heart?

II.

be my voice
we have fallen together
from the eyes of God

III.

sisters and brothers, conjugate
the only action accorded me by love:
to embrace your good and evil.
When these words bring you joy
they cease to be words and become my soul

Act 3

I.

The world will be a better place
when it is exactly how we imagine,

we imagine.

II.
the tiny pink flowers
appear on the blossom tree.

From *The Book of the Memory of the Stars*

I.
I broke, and then was held together at the soul
with a paperclip. My mother and father
destroy the universe in my name. They do not
own a house. They eat
leg of lamb, leg of wolf, leg of bone.

V.
In high school, I was captain of the stargazing squad.
3 times, the sun was a star.
My freshman year the sun was famous.
(dec, march, june): I was the famous sun, but

XII.
to this I now admit: I am not the sun. I
try & remember that time when in high school the sky
held the sun like a baby. I get out *The Book
of the Memory of the Stars*, written in the blood of
the paperclipped soul. Somewhere above me,
like a mosquito, the Angel of Mercy hovers, drooling
on my shoulder. The abusive light of the stars
suckles, suckles, suckles And the long dead
[members of my stargazing squad
appear on my shoulder

holding umbrellas, eating

leg of lamb, leg of wolf, leg of God; chanting with

their mouth's full,

the names of my parents, the names

of the stars, consummating the]

relationships we have with ourselves, they sing.

And God declared:
let there be mystery between you
until you know the sameness of every heart
inside your own heart.

Gratitude for Marcy and Julia, who overwhelmed my doubts with their enthusiasm. And for Paul and Lisa, who pointed my energies in constructive directions. And Jil, and Marcy again, for the cover that I had envisioned but couldn't express. And for Summer, who brought exemplary character and compassion and uncommon drive to a moment that would not have been miraculous without those contributions. And to the abyss, for being the emptiness that these things filled.

About the Author

Philip Jason is the author of the novel *Window Eyes* (Unsolicited Press, 2023). He has other poetry forthcoming from Shanti Arts Press. For more, please visit philipjason.com.

About the Press

Unsolicited Press is based out of Portland, Oregon and focuses on the works of the unsung and underrepresented. As a womxn-owned, all-volunteer small publisher that doesn't worry about profits as much as championing exceptional literature, we have the privilege of partnering with authors skirting the fringes of the lit world. We've worked with emerging and award-winning authors such as Shann Ray, Amy Shimshon-Santo, Brook Bhagat, Kris Amos, and John W. Bateman.

Learn more at unsolicitedpress.com. Find us on X (formerly Twitter) and Instagram.

www.ingramcontent.com/pod-product-compliance
Lightning Source LLC
Chambersburg PA
CBHW031422120626
46545CB00006B/2230